JACOBSON'S ORGAN

Other plays by Nicholas Corder

Cash and Carrie

Nigel's Wrist

Jacobson's Organ

Nicholas Corder

J. Garnet Miller

First published by J. Garnet Miller
(A division of Cressrelles Publishing Company Limited)
10 Station Road Industrial Estate, Colwall, Near Malvern, WR13 6RN
Telephone/Fax: (01684) 540154

A CIP record for this book is available from the British Library.

ISBN: 0-85343-639-8

Printed in the UK by Cressrelles Publishing Company Ltd.

Characters

Fiona Jacobson

- A young doctor in her mid-twenties

Nigel Struthers

- A post-graduate student of similar age

Scene

The action takes place in each of Fiona and Nigel's bedrooms and in a wine bar. Action is almost continuous.

The set serves as Fiona and Nigel's individual bedrooms, as well as the wine bar. The stage is bare, save for a table with two chairs. The table is split down the middle with one half for Fiona and half for Nigel, or two small tables can be used. Their actions should show that they are inhabiting two separate spaces in the first scene.

On Nigel's side of the table are the various items needed for him to prepare for his night out - roll-on deodorant, after-shave, spray-on body mist, large pack of condoms. There is also a book on snakes, a bottle of beer and a small, gift-wrapped package containing a rubber snake. His stuff is neat. The wine and glasses for the wine bar can be kept in a box next to Nigel's table. He wears a dressing-gown and smart casual wear suitable for a student going on a date

On Fiona's side are her equivalents - make-up, tissues, cotton wool, etc, including a large box of tampons. Both sides have the same copy of *Time Out* or the local equivalent listings magazine. She has a huge handbag that contains all sorts of things, including pen and paper, items of make-up, perfume, a very crumpled pack of condoms, envelope containing a letter. Her stuff is untidy. She has a bottle of vodka. She wears smart casual clothes fitting for a young woman going on a first date.

They also both have mobile phones.

Act I, Scene One

*The song "What Becomes of the Broken-hearted?" by Jimmy Ruffin plays. Enter **Fiona**, swaying to the music. She is mostly dressed, but needs to add some finishing touches. She sits and brushes her hair in time to the music, looks at herself in an imaginary mirror. She applies lipstick, then draws back her lips. She leans back to admire herself.*

Fiona: Mirror, mirror on the wall. *(Deciding she's overdone make-up.)* Who's the biggest slapper of all?
    She removes all the make-up and then begins to re-apply it.
Fiona (*As Mother*): "Far too much make-up, Fiona, you're getting slap happy." *(Herself.)* You get out of the habit, don't you. You get out of the habit of knowing just how much to put on to get it right. There's no-one there to guide you, to show you what to do. You spend all day talking to half-cut half-wits - and that's just the other staff - then you come home and start drivelling on into the ether. God help us. There might be some kind of alien life-form in a distant galaxy hanging round the radio receiver picking this up a zillion light years from now thinking this is the way we all behaved down here. I may not accomplish much in this life, but at least I know that when the little green men arrive and they're wearing too much make-up, chuntering to themselves and not getting enough sex, Fiona Jacobson will have been their rôle-model.
    She picks up the bottle of vodka and pours herself a slug.

1

Fiona: One for me . . . and . . . one for me for being such a good girl. *(Pours another slug.)* I shouldn't. You should see what this lot can do to you. Just like I do. Every day of the bloody week. Turn your liver into eleven kilos of rubber. Sod all use as an organ, but a boon if you're learning how to draw. God, it's dangerous living on your own. It's not the muggers, the buggers and the burglars, it's the constant threat of madness. *(As Mother.)* "Oh, there you go again - talking to yourself, Fiona." *(Herself.)* I shouldn't bring my work home with me. Hepatology's hardly a hoot. It's all piss-heads with Emmentaler livers. Come on, cheer up, you old bat. It's an evening full of tender promise. I've got the details in here somewhere. *(She roots through handbag and finds a crumpled pack of condoms. She studies them.)* That's definitely not it. *(Reads.)* "Use by November 2000". God. It seems like a different age. It is a different age. What's he called again? Neil? Norman? I'm sure it was 'N'. Nick? Nobby? Maybe Nobby's spelt with a 'K'? Nathan? Why are all names beginning with 'N' so bloody stupid?

She roots through handbag again and pulls
out envelope containing letter and reads.

Fiona: He's got nice clear handwriting. Mine looks like an explosion in an ink factory. Yes! I was right. Nigel. Currently writing up his doctoral thesis. Doesn't say what subject. Not a doctor yet. At least I pull rank. Football, cinema and reading.

Why is it if they've got testicles they like football? Assuming he has got testicles. It's probably just my luck to get some kind of wimp with a sperm count so low he could count them on the fingers of one hand and often does. *(As Mother.)* "Don't judge people, Fiona, until you get to know them."

Cinema - that's good. Or it might be. Just so long as he doesn't think *Bridget Jones* was a good film. All that crap about women being incapable of living on their own and having to have a man to be completely satisfied and drinking too much if they don't. *(She takes a drink.)* What a heap of shit.

Reading. Could be anything. Dick Francis or Dostoevsky. I hope it's not science fiction. Still, you can tell straight away. Beard equals science fiction. He doesn't mention a beard anywhere. Maybe it's not reading, but Reading. Perhaps he's got a fixation about Reading. He knows all the statistics. Population. Birth rate. Infant mortality statistics. Sunrise, sunset. All the names of the twin towns. Railway timetable. The time and number of the last bus to Marlow Bottom and the year it was first commissioned by Thames Valley Transport. He knows everything there is to know about Reading. In fact, he's come hot-foot from the latest *Dr. Who* convention at Reading. *(She has another drink.)*

Come on, Fiona! Why are you being so hard on the poor guy? It's no wonder you can't keep one long enough to bother changing the sheets. What's wrong with football, cinema and reading? It's more than most blokes. If they were honest, they'd put down getting pissed, shagging and farting, like Doug, the Flatulence King. It's hardly a crime. It's not like he's into arson and rubbing up against women on the Tube and sticking gerbils up film stars' arses.

We used to get that, you know. I worked in Accident and Emergency before I started to specialise in people who've drunk their livers into submission. A & E was a rich tapestry compared to hepatology. Every now and again, you'd get someone coming in with something lodged up their backside. All sorts of things. In six months I came across two Coca-Cola bottles, a long-handled hairbrush and an Action Man Scuba Diver. They all say "Oh, I just fell on it - by accident." How the hell can you fall on an Action Man Scuba Diver? And then get it lodged up your arse? He's in a rubber suit, for God's sake. You'd need a King Size tub of KY jelly to get it up there. Well, *queen* size, maybe.

What on earth would possess anyone to stick a rubber-clad scale-model fighting doll up their back passage? It's almost bound to get stuck, isn't it? Otherwise they'd equip it differently and call it Action Man Pot-holer. It wasn't getting the Action Man out that was hard, it was fishing round for the missing spear gun and half an aqualung. Bugger that.

Think positive. He's probably charming. He's Colin Firth. He's your very own Mr D'Arcy. Yuck. That's a bit Bridget Jonesy. Silly, sad, lonely bitch. But he is suave. Yes, he's suave. Sophisticated. Sexy. Football is an outlet for his male aggression. He understands the need to press the release valve on the old testosterone. It allows him to get in touch with his feminine side. He's cultured. He listens to Mozart and reads Jane Austen and he only watches films with subtitles, unless they're Fred Astaire films. In fact, he adores Fred Astaire, but was just too shy to say so on the form. And he dances just like him. That's more like it. So, there he is - suave, sophisticated, sexy and pure mercury on the dance floor. (*Raises her glass.*) Your very good health, Nigel.

"Three Lions" by The Lightning Seeds *as* **Nigel** *enters his side of stage, dancing clumsily, in a dressing-gown. He too sways along with his music, in a laddish fashion. He removes his dressing-gown in a ridiculous striptease to reveal that he is wearing only comedy boxer shorts and socks. He picks up his trousers and waves them above his head like a football scarf, chanting "Eng-ur-land" a couple of times, joining in on the "It's coming home", etc. He uses a roll-on deodorant, then uses it as a microphone for karaoke. He sprays body mist into air and walks under it, so that it falls on him. He dances around doing up his shirt. He complicates everything by constantly bopping around. He ostentatiously tries to fart, but with no success.*

Nigel: Could have sworn I needed one.

Nigel flattens out the book on the table in front of him. Slow fade of music in background.

Nigel: Jacobson's Organ. Never knew that. (*To audience.*) Did you? It's what snakes have. When they flick their tongues in and out, they're breathing and the little receptor inside the mouth is called Jacobson's Organ. Interesting, eh?

Nigel flicks his tongue in and out to test it.

Fiona: What if we've got nothing in common, though? I can't just talk about work. I've got to think of something else.

Nigel: Just boning up. Herpetology - snakes, reptiles, that kind of thing. It'll give us a starting point. A way to get chatting.

4

Nigel goes back to his book.

Fiona: I wonder what we could talk about. Not work. He doesn't want to know about work. Football. I hope he doesn't try to explain the off-side rule.

Nigel: Shit! Some of these pythons can grow to 10 metres in length. That's more-or-less from the goal-line to the penalty spot.

Fiona roots through her enormous handbag looking for pen and paper.

Nigel: Christ, that would be one hell of a trick.

Nigel examines his underwear to see if he could pull off the same trick.

Fiona: I hope he's not fixated by penis size.

Nigel: Well, Fiona, the old Struthers's one-eyed trouser snake can grow to quite considerable lengths . . . under certain conditions. *(In a macho voice.)* "In fact, I would go so far as to say that one of the difficulties I've always found in having such a large penis is what I like to call my underwear comfort zone. It's hard getting them with a pouch big enough."

Fiona: If he is, it probably means he's got a tiddly tadger.

Nigel (*Picks up condoms*): They were out of Jumbo Joy Jollyboys, so I had to make do with Wonderwhoppers instead. I hope you like raspberry flavour.

Fiona (*Wistfully*): When you get to see a lot of penises, you get to know the type. I don't mean the type of penis. I mean, there's not a sort of biological taxonomy of penises, like *Penis Neanderthalis, Penis Erectus* or *Penis Sapiens.*

Nigel: I thought about chocolate. But I was worried in case you might be a diabetic.

Nigel gets out one of the condoms and inflates it.

Fiona: No, I mean the type of man whose brains are in his dick. Most of the ones I see are of the variety known as *Penis Piccalilli* anyway. Loads of them. All shrivelled. Loads of them. Too many. A whole bunch of them. I wonder if that's what you call a group of penises? A bunch? They are a bit banana-shaped. No, I think it's a hand of bananas, isn't it. A hand of penises. They measure horses in hands. Four inches. Probably just my luck.

Nigel: I did hear you could get prawn cocktail-flavoured ones. Then it occurred to me you might have a seafood allergy. You can't say I'm not a considerate lover.

Fiona: A pride. A group. A parade. A flock. A flock of penises. So *that's* what the shepherds were watching by night! Yes, tending the flock had a completely different meaning in those days. No wonder the Angel of the Lord had to shine a light all around. *(As Gabriel.)* "All right, you shepherds, stop fiddling with your flocks." *(Herself.)* Nativity plays will never be the same again. God, Fiona, it's no wonder they've gone past their sell-by-date. I bet even men don't talk about penises this much.

Nigel: Now, I don't want you to think that all I ever talk about is the penis, but I do think it's worth mentioning what I think is its most impressive quality. I know what you're thinking, and you're wrong. It's the fact that you can piss wherever the hell you want. It means that the average man can piss on their own. They don't have to go to the bog in twos and threes. In fact, it's easier to piss when you're on your own. A handy little device the penis.

Fiona *(Exiting)*: Oh, no. It's nerves. I need a pee. I hope I don't have to keep on going all night. Oh, no. I'll have to go. It's the bloody drink. It's a diuretic.

Nigel: You can use the penis for all sorts of things. It's multi-purpose. It's kind of like a Swiss Army knife. But that pissing thing's the business. When I was at school, some joker took a big fat felt-tip pen and drew three horizontal lines above the urinal. And alongside, he wrote "national average", "school record" and "world record". Might become a craze. Outgrown your Newton's Cradle? Played out your Playstation? Then potter with your penis! Hours of endless fun, for all the family. Or at least the male members.

I don't want you to think I go on about penises all the time. I don't. It's just that they've got a rôle to play in life, haven't they? After all, they are the male reproductive organ. You can have as many ovaries as you like, but without those little tadpoles, you're just not going to get very far.

It must be quite sad for the old todger, waving goodbye to those little squiggles of DNA replicant. *(Waves.)* Keep your heads up lads and swim, boys, swim. Go to work on an egg.

Clever little gadget the old hooded serpent. They should sell them in the *Innovations* catalogue. I wonder if you could use it for getting stones out of horses' hooves.

And here's another thing - you can't have a sense of humour without one. That's why men are funnier than women and you can never joke with a woman who isn't getting any!

Nigel continues to get dressed whilst reading the book. There is the sound of a toilet flushing and **Fiona** *rushes back in.* **Nigel** *tries to put on a sock and falls over.*

Fiona: I could make a joke early on. That would lighten the atmosphere. Men like women with a sense of humour. It makes them think we're not frigid or desperate for sex.

Nigel: Perhaps it's best not to mention the wedding tackle. Don't want to put her off.

Fiona: Maybe we won't have to talk about anything. Maybe it'll be love at first sight.

Nigel: I'll go for steely and interesting. *(Practises different greetings.)* Hi, I'm Nigel. Hello, I'm Nigel. I'm Nigel.

Nigel pulls his underpants out of his bum crack and sniffs his hand. He holds out his hand as though to shake an imaginary hand.

Tchaikovsky's Romeo and Juliet - *the slushy bit - soars.*

Nigel: You must be Fiona.

Fiona: I've been looking forward to meeting you.

Nigel: I'm so pleased to meet you. You must be a model in your spare time.

Fiona: I feel as though I know you already. You never said how devastatingly handsome you were. You move just like Fred Astaire.

Nigel: I've been dying to meet you too. Fancy a shag? *(Girlish voice.)* Oh, you silver-tongued lothario, you've talked me into it already.

Fiona: I must be desperate.

Nigel: She's probably gagging for it.

Fiona *(Together)* : God, I need a drink.

Nigel   :

> *Nigel has a swig of beer, Fiona takes a slug of vodka.*

Fiona *(Reads)*: Football, reading, cinema. What the hell do I know about football, reading and cinema?

Nigel: No. You shouldn't expect too much on a first date.

Fiona: What do you talk about on a first date? *(As Mother.)* "You certainly don't ask him in for coffee, Fiona. In my day, coffee meant a hot beverage, not hank-panky in seven different and anatomically challenging positions with a complete stranger."

Nigel: Mind you, if you're coughing up the price of a few drinks, you should expect something. You know what I mean, lads. A bottle of Chardonnay's a bit of an investment, isn't it?

Fiona *(As Mother)*: "If you're too easy, he won't respect you." *(Herself.)* I'm not just talking to myself, I'm talking to myself in my mother's voice. I'm turning into Norman Bates. I've become one of those sad people who talk to themselves in silly voices.

Nigel *(In a macho voice)*: "Gonna give you lurv. Gonna give you joy. Gonna give you cystitis."

Fiona: If he's some kind of wet rag, it'll be up to me to drive the conversation.

Nigel: No, you shouldn't steer straight for the bedroom the first time. Play it cool.

Fiona: So what am I going to say? What the hell are we going to talk about? I know. I'll make a list. *(She gets a pen and paper from her bag. She is poised to write.)* So what *do* men want to talk about?

> *Fiona stares blankly at her pad. During **Nigel's** speech, she makes a few notes and them crosses them out.*

Nigel: I've got to learn to calm down. Women like a bloke who seems to be in charge of the situation. Got to relax. I bought this CD once. It was called "Relax to the Gentle Sound of the Blue Whale". Relax? It was all squeaks and gurgles. It drove me up the bloody wall. It was enough to make you cancel your Greenpeace subscription and send the money to the Japanese whaling fleet so they can get the job over and done with quicker.

How can you relax when Manchester United are always top of the bloody league? D'you know, there was some talk in the faculty about giving David Beckham a bloody honorary doctorate. I e-mailed my supervisor and said if I got myself a stupid haircut and a thick wife, could I skip writing up and they could just give me the PhD and save a load of hassle.

We could do work exchange. Becks can stare at a blank computer screen wondering what the hell he's been doing for the past two-and-a-half years and I'll fanny about in midfield, hogging all the free kicks. I wonder if I'd have to shag Posh? *(With relief.)* No, it's a job swap, not a life swap.

Nigel starts to play football with his inflated condom. He commits a bad foul.

Nigel *(Mimics Beckham)*: "What d'you mean late tackle? I got there as soon as I could." Hey hey. *(Himself.)* The old ones are the best. *(He turns to show the imaginary referee his shirt number. As Beckham.)* "Number 7, ref. Doctor Beckham." *(Looks at watch. Himself.)* Christ! I've only got a few minutes. Better knuckle down and learn a few more snippets to toss carelessly into the conversation. A few bons mots.

Nigel goes back to his book, swatting up.

Fiona: So, let's see what we've got. *(Reads from her list.)* Football, cinema, reading. I'm not making much progress here. It's hard on your own. Cracks start to appear, you know. My friend Jill reckons that I should Feng Shui the flat.

It's an odd business this Feng Shui. You have to do all sorts of things. Apparently, if you leave the toilet seat up, you lose a whole load of chi down the pan. I wonder what chi actually is. Obviously, men can't have any, cause they always leave the seat up. I'm not convinced, but Jill says it would help me to harmonise with my surroundings.

What on earth does she mean? Harmonise with my surroundings? Paint myself beige? Why don't I just teach the walls to talk to themselves. Don't need to teach them to drink, they're plastered already. Hey hey. The old ones are the best. This isn't getting me very far with my list, though.

They both pore over their respective tasks. Fiona taps her teeth with a pen. Nigel flicks at pages in the book.

Nigel: There are two kinds of snake poison - haemotoxic and neurotoxic. *(As Michael Caine.)* "Now, there's not a lot of people know that."

Fiona: Think, think, think.

Nigel: Haemotoxic are to do with blood-clotting. That makes sense.

Fiona: I wonder if he's got any pets?

Nigel: And neurotoxic. They paralyse the nerves.

Fiona: A cat. Yes. He's probably got a cat. If he lives on his own, he's bound to have a cat. It speaks of his feminine side.

Nigel stands up and pretends to suffer from neurotoxins.

Nigel *(Stiff upper lip, British colonial)*: "Can hardly move, Fiona. My pet pit viper Sidney got me. Thank God you're an expert."

Fiona: They used to burn women who lived on their own with cats as witches. Now they just give them little blue tablets, some Oddbins vouchers and a lifetime's subscription to *Cosmopolitan*.

Nigel *(Continues his charade)*: "I'm afraid it's in a very delicate place. What? You'll suck out the poison? But I hardly know you. This is so awfully kind of you. Ah yes, excellent."

Fiona: He's probably not done it in ages either. He probably has to get his mother to sew up his pockets just to stop him from playing with himself.

Nigel *(As a Master of Ceremonies)*: "What a way to go! A big warm welcome to Neil and Bob, not so much two good friends, more of an instruction!"

Fiona: I do hope he doesn't have strange fantasies.

Nigel *(Together)* : Shit, what's the time?

Fiona   :

They scrabble around making final preparations.
Their mobile phones ring simultaneously.

Fiona: Hello, Mother.

Nigel: Hello, Mother.

Fiona: Not much.

Nigel: Not much.

Fiona: I thought I'd just have a quiet night in. There's an old film on Channel 4.

Nigel: I thought I'd stay in and watch the football.

Fiona: No, Mother, I hadn't forgotten.

Nigel: No, Mother. How could I?

Fiona: No, there's no-one I'd like to bring. No, nobody at the moment.

Nigel: Of course I'll be on my own, Mother. How could I share your cooking with anyone else? *(To audience.)* Environmental Health would be on to me like a shot.

Fiona: No, I've not got anybody "lined up" either. *(To audience.)* Like I've got them queuing up for it.

Nigel: No, Mother. I'm not that way inclined.

Fiona: No, Mother. I like men, it's just that I don't have anyone in my life right now.

Nigel: Mother, if I were, don't you think I'd be called Russell or Julian or Quentin or Dale.

Fiona: Yes, I know Charlotte's like that, but have you ever seen me wearing dungarees or pork-pie shoes?

Nigel: I think Dale Winton is, Mother. He may say he isn't, but I think he is.

Fiona: OK, so she prefers to be called Charlie now. I don't care if she is or isn't. It's no big deal.

Nigel: Yes, I know you had doubts about Father, but I think he just liked the outdoor life.

Fiona: It's her choice, Mother. Not all of us want children.

Nigel: Scouting's just not in fashion any more.

Fiona: But not right now.

Nigel: Have you ever seen me going round IKEA on a Sunday picking out scatter cushions? Hey? That proves it. Anyway, nobody cares nowadays.

Fiona: Well, maybe. Women remain fertile well into their forties, you know.

Nigel: No, I'm not getting moody.

Fiona: No, I'm not getting broody.

Nigel: I've been busy working on my thesis.

Fiona: Well, I don't know. Someone at the hospital maybe.

Nigel: About six pages.

Fiona: If I don't meet someone before the biological clock stops ticking, I'll have artificial insemination by donor.

Nigel: No, I'm all right for cash. I've got a job lined up tomorrow.

Fiona: No, Mother. It was a joke. We have irony here, we're south of the irony curtain.

Nigel: No, I haven't forgotten.

Fiona: No, I won't be late.

Nigel *(Together)* : See you on Sunday.

Fiona   :

They hang up simultaneously.

Nigel *(As football commentator)*: "The boy Struthers looks on form tonight. He's been through a bit of a lean patch recently. What do you make of his chances, Barry?" *(As Barry.)* "Oh, he's a class act, Struthers. It's the longest he's been without scoring. His luck's got to change soon."

Fiona *(As Mother)*: "Fiona, what have you let yourself in for." *(Herself.)* Keep, quiet, Mother. Oh no, I'm not just imagining my mother speaking, I'm replying as well! I am going completely gaga. Who wants to be seen with an invisible mother on a blind date? That's it. I've finally cracked. Still, at least I've got the power to section myself under the Mental Health Act. It may come to that, yet.

They grab their respective copies of Time Out *(or equivalent). Nigel finishes his beer, whilst Fiona has another slug of Vodka. They both stand sideways. She examines her bosom and backside, straightens her skirt. He smoothes down his shirt. Both decide that something is amiss. Nigel stuffs a hankie down his pants. Fiona pulls up her boobs and sticks cotton wool in her bra.*

Nigel: You're gorgeous.

Fiona: You'll do.

Nigel puts the gift-wrapped package in his pocket. Exeunt.

Lights out.

12

Scene Two

A couple of hours later. Music - Tom Jones and the Stereophonics "Mama Told Me Not to Come". Fiona hurtles into her half of the set, throwing down her handbag & coat.

Fiona: What a disaster. What a complete and utter disaster. Men! *(She finds the vodka and pours herself a bit more. As Mother.)* "Well, what do you expect, Fiona, if you will go around on blind dates. I told you it wasn't a great idea." *(Herself.)* Oh, shut up, Mother. If I didn't have to carry you around as extra psychological baggage, maybe I wouldn't have irrational bloody phobias in the first place. Men! They're not from Mars, they're from Uranus.

Fiona starts taking off make-up etc. Nigel storms into his half of the room. He is holding a bloody handkerchief to his nose.

Nigel: Women! *(He pours himself a beer.)* They're just not rational human beings. You go out of your way to show them little acts of kindness and they throw a bloody wobbler.

Fiona: What a complete and utter cock-up. What on earth possessed him to do something like that?

Nigel examines his nose in the imaginary mirror.

Nigel: I think it might be broken.

Fiona: They just don't think.

Nigel: What the hell did I do? We're not dealing with logical, rational thought here.

Fiona: How could he ruin it like that? And he seemed so nice to begin with.

Nigel: She seemed all right at first.

They begin re-enacting a flashback of their meeting.

Nigel: Fiona:?

Fiona: Neil?

Nigel: Nigel.

Fiona: Nigel. I'm sorry. I meant Nigel.

13

Nigel: Don't worry. It's an easy enough mistake to make. After all, they both begin with the letter "N".

Fiona: Like Nick or Norman or Nobby.

Nigel: Nobby could begin with a "K" though.

Fiona: I was thinking that too.

Nigel: It's telepathy.

Fiona: I knew you were going to say that.

Nigel: Chardonnay?

Fiona: Fantastic. My favourite. Although I confess I had a couple of vodkas before I came out. Dutch courage.

Nigel: Me too. Beer.

Fiona: You look quite normal.

Nigel: Beer drinkers are human too.

Fiona: I mean you don't look like someone on a blind date.

Nigel: Damn it, I knew I should have worn that carnation!

Fiona: I mean, you haven't got two heads. Although they do say two heads are better than one.

Nigel: Not if you're trying to buy a pullover.

Fiona: I kept on rehearsing what I was going to say.

Nigel: Same here.

Fiona: I had imaginary conversations.

Nigel: I do running commentaries. You know. Like the football.

Fiona: Of course. Football, cinema and reading. I've found myself doing it a lot recently.

Nigel: Which one? Football, cinema or reading?

Fiona: Talking to myself. I even had imaginary conversations about how this date would go.

Nigel: So did I. It must be a full moon or the vernal equinox.

Fiona: God. It's so nice to meet someone with a brain for a change. Better than the slimy creeps I get to work with.

Nigel: I always thought they were dry.

Fiona: They are - but sometimes they can't keep it up.

Nigel: What?

Fiona: Let's not talk about work.

Nigel: No. Quite. So, in your imaginary conversation, how did the date go?

Fiona: D'you want me to be honest?

Nigel: Not very well then.

Fiona: It was a disaster.

Nigel: OK, so apart from the two heads.

Fiona: No, it wasn't that. I just thought you'd be some creepy little guy.

Nigel: You wouldn't be the first woman to think that.

Fiona: Oh, no, Nigel, don't say that.

Fiona *(To audience)*: So you see, I thought things were going pretty well. We seemed to have a lot in common.

Nigel *(To audience)*: She seemed great. Pretty. Good sense of humour. I couldn't believe my luck. Not a hint of what was to come.

Fiona *(To audience)*: You can't always tell though, can you? He seemed really nice. He didn't even talk about football. He was a good laugh.

They return to one another.

Fiona: Why is it that men like football?

Nigel: Oh, come on, you're just trying to humour me. You don't want to know about football.

Fiona: No, you're right;. I don't.

Nigel: Although the off-side rule can be pretty fascinating.

Fiona: Really? *(Realises he's pulling her leg.)* Oh, you bugger. No, whatever you do, don't try explaining it to me, not unless you want me to attempt suicide by drowning myself in a half-empty glass of Chardonnay.

Nigel *(Pours a drink)*: You'd better have some more.

Fiona *(To audience)*: You see. It seemed so perfect. It was almost as though he knew exactly what I wanted.

They turn their attentions back to one another.

Fiona: Have you been here before?

Nigel: Is that the blind date variation of do you come here often?

Fiona: No, I mean, have you been in this wine bar before?

Nigel: I'm not really a wine bar person. I prefer pubs.

Fiona: So do I. Nice country pubs.

Nigel: With a choice of seven real ales.

Fiona: And a big log fire.

Nigel: The trouble is they're always full of stockbrokers wearing Arran sweaters, pretending to be farmers.

Fiona laughs.

Nigel *(To audience)*: Even when my jokes weren't very funny she laughed. It was so easy-going. It didn't seem like a first date.

Fiona *(To audience)*: Yes, he's right. Normally you just end up chit-chatting about little things, but we really seemed to click, didn't we?

Nigel: Oh, yes.

Fiona: We even got onto the subject of old flames. *(Getting tipsy and addresses Nigel.)* Who's the worst girlfriend you ever had, Nigel?

Nigel: You promise not to laugh if I let you in on a secret?

Fiona: Cross my heart.

Nigel: This is the first time I've ever been out with a girl.

Fiona *(Shocked)*: Really? *(Then realising.)* Oh, you bugger. You've done it again. All right. I'll tell you about mine then.

Nigel: You go in for girls as well? This is getting better by the minute. You haven't got a friend who might like to join us?

Fiona: Now don't be k-naughty, K-nigel! I had this boyfriend called Doug. He used to fart in bed.

Nigel: Everyone farts in bed.

Fiona *(Mock outrage)*: I don't. I may break wind, but I certainly do not fart. He used to lift up the duvet so he could smell them.

Nigel: I still don't see what's wrong with that.

Fiona: He used to make me smell them as well.

Nigel: Sometimes you can't help it. They just, you know, seep out. Like swamp gas.

Fiona: Yes, but he wanted me to grade them.

Nigel: You're kidding. What - A,B,C or something?

Fiona: It was awful. He had a sliding scale that went from stale cabbage to Agent Orange.

Nigel: Was he sick?

Fiona: No, but I was.

Nigel: I'm not surprised.

Fiona: I chucked him out when he wanted me to start lighting them. You can't be too sure if some of this bed-linen is flame-proof or not.

Nigel: How long did he last.

Fiona: Several eggies, six chloroforms and an SBD. By the third night I couldn't stand it. I spent nearly thirty quid on pot pourri when he left. I'm still not sure if the smell's gone. So, what about you?

Nigel: I guess mine must smell a bit, but I don't think I'm actually proud of them.

Fiona: Girlfriends! Who was your worst ever girlfriend?

Nigel: I've not really had that many.

Fiona: Oh, come on, Nigel, with your sphincter control you must have had dozens. There must be at least one where you thought "what the hell am I doing with her?"

Nigel: I don't think I've ever had that much choice.

Fiona *(To audience)*: And his honesty. I liked the fact that he didn't seem full of bullshit. He wasn't putting it on. It was kind of refreshing.

Nigel *(To audience)*: Maybe I should have tried to be a bit more macho and invented some story. Women go for that sometimes. But I liked her, so I didn't want to pretend. *(To Fiona.)* I suppose there was Jenny Threadgold.

Fiona: What was so weird about Jenny then?

Nigel: Look, I know you've told me yours, but do you mind if I don't tell you mine.

Fiona: Did she hurt you then, Nigel?

Nigel: Kind of.

Fiona: I'm sorry. *(To audience.)* And I was. I believed him, but you should never sleep with anyone on a first date.

Nigel *(To audience)*: I thought I was going to score. And on a first date!

Fiona *(To Nigel)*: I don't sleep with men on a first date.

Nigel: I understand. *(To audience.)* Shit!

Fiona: But I might well do on a second one.

Nigel: Yes, I understand. *(To audience.)* Shit!

Fiona: Would you like to ask me out on a second date, then?
Nigel: You mean it? A second date?
Fiona: Yes, I do. Like this is date number one - we could go on date number two.
Nigel: So, if we went on a second date, then you might sleep with me? *(To audience.)* Shit!!
Fiona: No wonder you're an academic. Sharp thinking like that. You catch on fast.
Nigel: When you say "sleep", you mean . . .
Fiona: Provided you don't try to explain the off-side rule or grade your flatulence.
Nigel: If I do, I'll use the Greek alphabet to make it seem more intellectual. Alpha, Beta . . .
Fiona *(Mock stern)*: I mean it.
Nigel: Really?
Fiona: Yes, really.
Nigel: If I went away for a few minutes and came back, would that count as a second date?
Fiona: It's not that I'm not tempted, but I don't think that counts. And let's go to a pub next time.
Nigel: With a log fire.
Fiona: And seven real ales
Nigel: Where we can burn all the stockbrokers in Arran sweaters.
Fiona: But let's not stay out too long. We don't want to lose the focus of the evening.
Nigel: I don't know what to say.
Fiona: I've just offered you my fabulous, body beautiful on a plate. The least you could do is say "thank you".
Nigel: Thank you. Oh, I nearly forgot. I bought you a present.
Fiona: For me?
Nigel: Yes, it's a silly little thing really.
Nigel hands over the little gift-wrapped package.
Fiona: Chardonnay, witty talk and a little present. Perhaps you should disappear for a couple of minutes then come back and we'll call it our second date.
Nigel: Just open it. It's to do with your work.

Fiona: It's not some chopped liver?

Nigel: What?

Fiona: Only I can't see what else you could give a hepatologist.

Nigel: Hepatologist?

Fiona opens the wrapper and produces the snake. She starts laughing, then laughter turns to tears and back to more manic laughter.
She is suddenly very sober. Terrified.

Fiona: It's a fucking snake. I hate snakes.

Nigel: I'm sorry.

Fiona: What on earth would you want to give me something like that for?

Nigel: It's just a little joke.

Fiona: I hate snakes. How could you do this?

Nigel: It's just a rubber snake.

Fiona: God, if you wanted to put me off, you couldn't have come up with anything better.

Nigel: I thought you were a herpetologist. You know, snakes and lizards and things.

Fiona: This is worse than grading farts, Nigel. I'm going now, Nigel. Don't come after me.

Fiona exits.
Music - Van Morrison "Someone Like You" starts up.

Nigel: Fiona! *(Nigel starts off after her.)* Fiona:!

Nigel returns forlornly to centre stage. He picks up the snake and puts it back in his pocket.

Nigel: Bugger. It was all going so well. *(To audience.)* I thought we were really compatible. I thought we could have got something going then. It was meant to be a little joke. *(He pulls out his information sheet from his pocket.)* I thought it said "herpetologist". Snakes and lizards and . . . we all want a little warmth.

Fiona returns.

Nigel: You came back.

Fiona: I just wanted to say this. I'm tired of being let down by men. You meet someone and you get on really well. You think there are possibilities - moonlight walks, boat rides on the lake, Chinese take-aways whilst watching *ER*. You think that life's

19

going to change for the better. You've got someone to share it all with. We all need someone to look after us, Nigel. You think you've met someone really nice, then you look down and you see they've got feet of clay. I didn't think you'd have feet of clay, Nigel. I honestly thought you were different.

Nigel: I misread the information.

Fiona: I know, Nigel. Sometimes it's hard to read the signs.

Fiona moves towards him. Nigel holds out his arms as though offering a hug/kiss. Fiona rounds on Nigel and hits him. Nigel reels.

Nigel: What the hell was that for?

Fiona: For not being able to read the signs.

Nigel: It was the hand-writing. It was hard to tell what it said.

Fiona: So, it's my fault, then?

Nigel: It's just one of those things. A mistake.

Fiona: So, I'm a mistake, now?

Nigel (*Pulls out the snake*): You could have written a bit clearer. Look, it's a kid's toy. A little rubber snake.

Fiona shrieks again.

Fiona: You bastard!

Fiona delivers a second great punch. Nigel drops to his knees, clutching his face, pulling out a hankie. There is blood everywhere. Fiona storms off. Nigel gropes around on the floor. He staggers to his feet.

Nigel: I suppose a shag's out of the question then?

Curtain